Tenacity

Courage to Live, to Die, and to live again

Kenneth Lee Forbush

WESTBOW
PRESS®
A DIVISION OF THOMAS NELSON
& ZONDERVAN

WestBow Press books may be ordered through booksellers or by contacting:

WestBow Press
A Division of Thomas Nelson & Zondervan
1663 Liberty Drive
Bloomington, IN 47403
www.westbowpress.com
844-714-3454

ISBN: 978-1-6642-4668-3 (sc)
ISBN: 978-1-6642-4667-6 (e)

Print information available on the last page.

WestBow Press rev. date: 04/13/2022

Contents

Dedication

This is a book about my wife, Paula, who had a wonderful zest for life, an unstoppable drive to overcome all obstacles, a stubborn joy in the face of suffering, and a deep faith in God.

I dedicate this book to all the people whose lives she touched, and to those who did not know her, but who will be impacted by reading her story. In it, you will see true courage and determined struggle, as well as a zealous drive to make people happy. It was this drive, and her faith in God, that carried her on, until in His love, He led her home.

Introduction

Knowing Paula was a great gift, yet knowing her also led me into one of the hardest journeys of faith I have ever traveled. She was my wife. She was also the only woman that loved me, as a man wants to be loved. Marrying at a relatively late age for the first time, I was both cursed and blessed by not having had many ladies in my life. There were a few, but as usually happens they came and they went. Even those encounters were few and far in between.

But after 45 years of searching, waiting, and learning, the Lord put a wonderful woman into my life. It wasn't until I went on a contra dance weekend without her that I knew I needed her. Contra dancing was my favorite pastime. It was fun because I was able to dance with as many women as I could stand, and they were all beautiful! I thrived on dancing. But on this weekend away from Paula, after a few years of being together, I felt virtually alone in the crowd. What was it about her that made me alive, which filled my days with completeness and love? As a Christian man, I know love. The love of Jesus is not virtual. It is as real as the air I breathe. I know His touch, His words of sweet comfort. But there was something special about Paula.

Very soon after that weekend, I asked her to marry me.

She said yes.

Imagine, if you can, the mixture of great joy and enormous stress that came upon me all of a sudden. This was serious business. I was making a promise that was going to be forever as long we both lived. I was no longer alone, having only myself to worry about. Everything I would say, do, and act upon had an impact on her, and I loved her, maybe more than myself. I had no Idea what I was getting myself into. Yet on my short adventure with her on this earth, in-time, I grew and changed in ways that were inconceivable at the time I that I proposed and she accepted.

She is now out-of-time. I miss her very much. What I am about to describe will show you a woman of faith, a stubborn woman, a very self-reliant woman, and yet so profoundly fragile. Prone to pain, to discouragement, and even depression, she never gave up. She was **tenacious**. On February 23, 2013 the melanoma cancer took her body, but never, I say NEVER, took her spirit. It never took her will to help and be there for her family, for her friends, and . . . for me.

To her very last breath, she showed love and courage. I know. I was there. So were her beautiful daughters. For my part, I not only felt her love, but her joy in going to see Jesus. She only hung around as long as she did to help us, so we would not have to hurt. (Oh, the hurt....) She is still with those who know her. This book will help you understand that in a real world, full of life and also full of pain, we can be strong, we can have hope, and that we absolutely need faith in Jesus, our Savior.

One

Inspiration and Reflection

One of our favorite preachers was a popular Sunday morning preacher. We watched him together every Sunday, and went to see one of his crusades in the LA Area. Paula gave me one of his books, after she'd read it herself. In that book she underlined and marked various thoughts and readings that spoke to her heart and touched her spirit. But the WAY she underlined them was different than I was accustomed to. Instead of merely underlying an entire sentence, she underlined and highlighted partial statements. She cherry picked concepts and ideas, hopes and expectations, and expressed regrets and pains through the clutter of excess words and phrases. The words she highlighted revealed her heart and mind. I was given a rare opportunity to see what my wife was thinking, and as I read those words I recalled events and experiences we were undergoing. I could literally relive a good or bad experience, and see why she thought that a point in the book, at that particular time, was so important. She always said she had a difficult time expressing herself. So she was usually silent. She, like a lot of us, was fearful of being misunderstood. Being misunderstood is not so distressing if the idea we are expressing is not very important. But an idea, a firm belief that is secured to your very heart and soul, is something that we guard very carefully, not allowing it to escape our inner selves if there is even the slightest chance of its being misunderstood. No, we keep it to ourselves. If we know God, we entrust these thoughts to Him, and to no one else.

So I was presented with this book, and with it, the rare opportunity to read her recorded thoughts, treasured affirmations, struggles, and victories. I knew that I was, in part, a reason she went through some of the struggles. I had no idea how to take care of another human being, someone I loved and who loved me. Years later, I don't think I was any closer to understanding, but I did know how to cause pain, and regret. And yet the love we had for each other, and our common love and faith in God, always brought us through and beyond those "life experiences".

I once heard that people say they want to "LIVE AND EXPERIENCE LIFE". But often times, they do not take into account the variety of experiences that life brings. When we are very young, we may see life as a continual party, or an adventure. Eventually and inevitably, the rude awakening will come - It's also painful, even in areas that bring joy. For most of us to be birthed into the world, our mothers endured pain. When the pain of labor is over, it gives way to happiness, and the mother holds her wonderful baby, a person with unlimited potential. Far from being simply the sum of all the parties and excursions into which we escape, some seasons of life can be dull, painful, and full of people who will hurt us, especially those closest to us.

My Paula was, in all ways, just like everyone else. She was ordinary, lived a normal life, worked every day, and loved her family and friends. But my Paula was also just like everyone else in this way - she was extraordinary. She had the power and conviction it took to make things happen, and even if they did not work the first, second, or 30th time, she never gave up.

I am going to share with you her own inspiration to be thankful, to become willing to get back up after a fall, and to help herself to release her pains to the One who loved her so very much, until she would go to be with Him. There are so many insights she gained, that she was able to pass on. I will try to express a few of them, but I expect that you will find many more arising within your own heart and soul. It is my hope that you, too, will find the courage and love to overcome, to learn, to become better, and to use the flaws that we all have as stepping stones to God's wisdom and be tenacious in your faith.

Two

Adventurous in Faith

The church we attended together made declarations over our lives. Often these declarations defied the outward circumstances we faced. She desired the very best, (and that did not necessarily mean the most expensive.) God gave her many talents, and among them were sewing, crafting and decorating. When she finished a project, you knew that every stitch was correct, and every measurement was precise. The clothes she made will last forever.

The following was a project for her. ***"I am not giving up! I have a gift from God, and I will not let it go."*** meant that at that very moment she had made up her mind, right then and there, that 'now' was the time to begin not settling for suffering, regret, or reliving painful experiences; In short- for an unsatisfactory and incomplete "helping of happiness". On the other hand she would lament how she was suffering and wanted to accomplish when she was discouraged, but she always came back to her determined self to move on and be strong.

I would see this decision manifest itself quite often. She and I would have our "days" when the helping of happiness was wanting, and the days would go on for more "days". I would usually be the privileged man to hear about these days, and to be shown how they digressed from the goal of the fullest helpings of peace, joy and happiness. Many times I would be the cause, or felt I was the cause of the difficulties we encountered with one another, and as hard as I tried to make things better, I seemed only made those worse. The phone calls during lunch breaks, the little things I tried to do to make her happy, were rejected. There was a point when I would have enough, and the next time I was going to confront her with "hard love". I wasn't going to take it anymore. But as soon as I made my mind up in this matter, I would get a call from her, and she would have no comprehension about why I was upset. She would be as nice and as beautiful a woman as you can imagine. She was kind, gentle and very loving. At those moments she had reached her full potential with God, Who had made her portion of happiness complete. If you are struggling to connect, in love, with a spouse or loved one who is physically or emotionally in pain, and feeling frustrated and helpless, I want to encourage you here to simply persist in loving. It may appear to you that your love is not being received, or even not wanted, but truly, no love is ever wasted. People who are gravely ill, or facing death, often need to turn inward to take hold of the last dregs in their reserves of strength, and it may become difficult for them to respond, even to those who love them most. But your love nourishes those reserves of strength in ways you cannot see. Your love lays up treasure in heaven. As you doggedly persevere through all the obstacles in your life and hang on as God leads you higher, you will indeed find your perfect portion of the happiness that lasts.

She would say *"I always talked to God as a real person and sometimes I was mad at him."*

My guess is that as Paula dealt with her life circumstances, she and God probably had it out together many times over this quote, even as we know Jacob wrestled with God, saying, "I will not let go until you bless me." When we are in the midst of the fire and cannot see beyond it, our decision to trust unwaveringly in God's goodness and faithfulness gives us a fierce hope that cannot be burned. Paula was not one to give up.

Paula was very good at reminding me of times I was faltering in my faith. I could be negative at times as I wish for better circumstances.

"You must keep your hopes up." This is a mantra that we often repeat to ourselves when our hope was down. So we declare, and receive as a command, "You MUST get your hopes up". This is not a suggestion, or a wish upon a falling star. For anything less than full commitment to the hope God has for us does not do Him justice. He is fully committed to our good, and we must be fully committed to receiving it. Paula knew God was in control. (Even if she did argue with him about the specifics).

When I met her at church, she was in the midst of being removed from the property where she lived. She had been falsely accused of tempting an older gentleman, and his wife did not appreciate that. My wife's heart was broken by this false accusation, and she and wanted to be with her friend who lived on the same property, but because of this she was unable to stay. She ended up in a local camp ground, living in a camping trailer that she was able to borrow at the last minute. For my part I was ignorant of the background politics at the time. I only knew that she had moved. To Paula's credit, she was upbeat, she was happy, and was content to be in her new surroundings. She did, indeed, hold her head up high, believing only what God said about her.

Paula was all about adventure. She had recently moved from California, with two dogs, two big dogs. She visited family on the way to North Carolina, and was staying with a lifelong friend, she shopped at the dollar store, at the cheapest grocery store, or market as she called it, and was able to get a job very quickly at her dream occupation. She worked at JoAnn's. She was a seamstress and craft person. She saw that God had her best interest in mind, despite the painful circumstances that had forced of her move. Whenever I saw her, we had great times together and that campground became her home. When she wasn't working, she was walking. Paula would walk for miles with her two dogs. She loved them both, even if they would give her trouble from time to time. Since she walked them by herself, she had two dogs and she had to control, which did not always work out well, since there are trees in North Carolina. And often the two dogs would get tangled up. But she was a great sport, and was never afraid of any new challenge. Her life itself proclaimed "you must never give up".

Her sense of adventure, simplicity and faith is what attracted me to her, not to mention that she was beautiful.

Three

Trips and adventures

Doc Hollywood

One of Paula's favorite movies was Doc Hollywood. It was about a jet setting young doctor on his way to become a plastic surgeon in the big city. His fancy car crashed as he was driving through some country roads into a field. He had to wait for his car to get repaired, but he was also taken into court and had to serve community service for the damage he did. His service was being a doctor to the community. As he gets to know the community and falls in love with a lovely girl, he starts to become a different person. When it comes time for his release he has a hard time leaving, but he does leave. After some time he finds the city life shallow and goes back to the country town. That was Paula. She loved the country.

One of the trips we took was to a town in Virginia. In the credits of the movie this town was mentioned, so we took a very long day trip to see it. She was as excited as a little girl. We got the maps and the directions to this city, but it has grown since then. After some investigation we were able to find the café that Michael Fox taped the movie. It was still a lot like the movie portrayed. We had a small meal and we went back home.

I tell this story to illustrate both her interest in seeing things, and her love of country life. That trip was also a spontaneous trip. She was a free spirit and she proved that when I had to stop on the way home to take a small nap. At least she know I would eventually make it home safely.

Route 40 at the end/beginning

Wilmington. North Carolina is the east coast Hollywood. Many scenes for movies are filmed in Wilmington. Of course Paula and I have been there many times and walked around the streets, and on the beaches. But one trip comes to mind that helps define Paula's life and death. Route 40 starts/end in Wilmington North Carolina. It end/starts in Barstow, California. The road runs continuously for 2554 miles. If you start in North Carolina, you will cross over fields and the smooth mountains of western NC and eastern Tennessee. The road goes into valleys and rugged mountains in the western states till it runs its course in a vast desert landscape. At Barstow California it ends at Interstate 15, a mere interstate. But in North Carolina. it continues under a state route and runs through Wilmington till it comes to a smaller town. One year we took that trip. It was during the slow time of the year between Christmas and the New Year. As usually happens, we always found something sublime and beautiful. The town was nearly empty. It looked like a town evacuated because it was haunted. The street decorations were homemade and we had to laugh at one sign that had a snowman's face on it that looked more like a Halloween decoration. But what did we find? We found a place that was quiet, a place that had small boats on the docks, and perhaps a few alligators. It was eerily quiet. The air smelled like the fish and shrimp that was its cargo.

In the summer this place was undoubtedly busy with boat traffic, with commerce and tourist. But Paula and I were not the typical tourist. We shared a time together to see that the end of the road was just an end of a road. No celebration. Just a quiet place that had memories and odors of life. How did we end up there? At her suggestion I followed her question. What's down there? Where does it lead? She was always looking to find out where the roads went. We found out that this long interstate highway started and ended in a quiet place, full of history, and mystery.

Four

Knowing Paula

Museums and oddities and sewing

One of the first local travels we took after we started dating was going to see museums and artistic creations in the local area. Our trips weren't to exotic islands, or sunny resorts. We lived in paradise. Why would we want to leave? Paula was only in North Carolina a short time before she explored the little hometown museums and oddities.

Among places we went to see was a medical/ nursing museum. We visited the museums in Raleigh, and all over the country. My Paula was a reader when it came to visiting the museums. She knew a lot more about an area or subject than when she came. At the battle fields of the civil war, she would read, and I took pictures. One place that she was very excited about was a windmill farm.

The windmills and sewing

A man lost his daughter. And he was an artisan of metal. He took scrap metal, large and small and built a working windmill in her honor. He painted it, and if you happen to be driving out on a lonely Carolina country road you would spot it on an overgrown corner. How Paula found this place is a mystery to me, except to say that God knew the desire of her heart and led her to it. He did not stop at one windmill.

The windmills he created were not the run of the mill regular and same size blades on a wheel. The first one told a story of his daughter. He welded pieces of this and that together, and by gazing at the windmill you learn of her life. The others that followed were engineering marvels. From 5 feet to 60 feet high his creations included Dutchmen sawing a log as the blades turned, and many items that looked more like music boxes, with small figures dancing. He had acres of them. We were privileged to visit with him. His work shop was a cluttered mishmash of iron, small and gigantic. His tools were simple. Yet out of a simple work shop, simple tools, and a simple man, great marvels of engineering were created and put on display.

Paula was a simple country girl, who had her own trade and tools. It wasn't gigantic structures she built. She made clothes. She started when she was a young girl. Her impetus was the need for better clothing at school. She and her brother were raised in poverty. That background made her a simple woman. The desire to better herself came from within. She wasn't satisfied with what poverty had to offer, so she learned to sew.

There may be a lot of great seamstresses but I would venture to say she was the best. There was something inside her that always pushed her to be better, to know more things, to learn and be motivated to do great things. When she started a project she wasn't finished till every stitch and add on was perfect. Unfortunately that also meant she had a lot of unfinished projects. She would start with the preparations and wait till she had time. So many times the deadline for what she really wanted to do would come up sooner that she wanted.

It may be the case that some projects were not completed, but for her grandchildren she made time. An example of this is the Halloween Costumes she made for the grandkids in California and for the grandkids in Missouri. Of course the kids had to have *her* costumes, for store bought ones weren't right. But as Halloween approached, the costumes were planned, the fabric meticulously picked out, but it was still a pile of fabric. That's when Paula was at her best. The last minute. She went into action and did not sleep for days, but she was busy measuring, cutting, sewing, tearing out mistakes, and building memories for our grandchildren. Her creations will always be treasured, and they will last till the grandkids grow up and their kids will wear them. Her work is that good.

Her insistence upon excellence, despite the obstacles she faced, was always apparent. When she was discouraged, a flurry of her tenacity rushed in, as in the case of costume building. Paula was responsible for dance companies outfits, for wedding outfits of her daughters, for her own wedding dress.

Her wedding dress was beautiful. Every bead, and other small balls of glass, (she had a name for them all) was sewn with care. In the end she delegated stringing the items together. And she put the finished products on her masterpiece. She was working on that dress the night before we were married. But that wasn't the only garment she worked on. She tailored the shirts and pants of the wedding party. Needless to say, I did not see much of her prior to our wedding day. That was ok, I took care of a lot of other details, and I had a lot of help. Her daughter came from Missouri and was a tremendous help. She, too, inherited the quality of doing only the best work.

The museums, the windmills, the placards in the battle fields, were all examples of Paula learning, and contributed to her learning to overcome impossible odds. Her sewing, from the beginning to her last project, were also examples of learning, and overcoming impossible time constraints with meticulously desired details. Paula was an untiring force that cared, that struggled, and overcame.

Finding a place of our own

An example of how remaining positive yields great rewards came when we were finally able to get a place of our own after moving to in California. There were great challenges to overcome; financial, emotional, familial, and personal. Only by trusting God and being determinedly positive did we reach the other side of these mountains.

We were having to accept the hospitality of her family for a couple years when we moved there from North Carolina. We appreciated the welcome, of course, but it was hard on Paula. Understandably, she wanted a place of her own. Unfortunately she wanted to buy a house when the market was at the top of a housing bubble. We learned we were "eligible" to get a loan on a house that would have used about 65% of our disposable income. The loan was interest only, and it was at a low introductory rate. She so wanted to have a house. It broke my heart to go to the homes we looked at, knowing they were way overpriced. Furthermore, we had just recently made a major car purchase that put us into more debt than I cared to be in. But I went along with her, until one day I'd had enough. We were on the freeway, and she was continuing to try to convince me that buying was the way we should go. Something inside of me had enough. Without being cruel, I spoke as plainly as I could to the woman I loved. I told her that if we got into another debt that I couldn't manage I would walk away. I don't normally speak so bluntly to anyone, most especially my wife. She was the wisest person in our relationship, and I knew that. But in this matter, she was not right. History proved my judgment to be correct in this matter. A few years later, people who took advantage of the same loans, and various other schemes offered in the housing market, lost their dreams, and suffered far more than if they had waited. I am fearful that I broke her heart at that moment, but from then on, we stopped looking for house to buy. Instead we looked for houses we could rent, at a rate we could afford. That house came along in a providential way, and we lived in it, with our dog, for many years. We had reached the goal. We were so happy to have a place of our own! I remember telling the family and friends who helped us move, "I am using MY KEY to open MY door." Some at this point may say that it wasn't mine, as it was rented. To that, I say that it was ours to use, and we no longer had to live under someone else's roof. Her daughter's family had their home all to themselves, and now, we had ours to ourselves as well.

Paula was very proud of our home. When she took an interior decorating class, she used our house as a model. That was the house our oldest grandson called the "fun house". It was the house in which our visiting grandchildren stayed overnight. It was the house we would come "home" to after work and after our trips, and where Paula and I would have beautiful holiday meals, just the two of us. That house had the garage that housed years and years of her sewing and crafting material. A two car garage stuffed with anything but cars. She was kind, and let me have one wall so that I could have a work bench.

The yard was the yard that the grandchildren played in. That same yard had the small inflatable bouncer they loved, and was our favorite spot to camp out at with them. That yard that was dug up, with the dirt from it landing in the kitchen as the grandkids came in from playing in the mud (created when they would play with the hose). It was the yard Paula and I then fixed up, making it a place where grass would grow and the kids did not bring more mud into the house!

Yes, we had a place of our own. A home where we could be ourselves, and have our privacy, and our times alone together. It did not come right away, but after some struggles, disappointments, and yes, even a broken heart. It came because we knew God had the best plan in mind, and we had to wait upon Him. Without knowing that He favored us, perhaps thinking that simple people like ourselves could not expect to have anything so nice, (so well, we'll just settle for this or that) we may have given up. How sad that would have been?

'If I believe for God's best, I know he will give them to me.' This was a common theme in her life

For Paula, these kinds of declarations served as nourishment to keep her spirit strong, and a guiding light to keep her eyes focused on her goal.

Jesus the source of hope

But declarations alone aren't enough. They serve the purpose of brining clarity to our minds in times of uncertainty. They can act as life rings to hang on to, when we feel lost in an ocean of fear or doubt. But a life ring without a Savior is useless. Paula knew the Savior; she knew Jesus, and that was most evident at the time of her new birthing into Jesus's arms. But it wasn't always that way. She came to know God by degrees of personal growth. For many years she stayed away from an active life of faith because she felt disconnected from God, and did not realize the greatness of His love for her until later in life.

We met in church. She told me how she used to avoid church because of marriage regulations that had been imposed on her, how she felt that since she had broken them, she was no longer good enough to go to church. But she had a realization that changed her. Faith wasn't about the rules. Faith was about the love of God for her, and her love for Him. It was the true love of God that drew her to the Catholic Church. A Franciscan priest showed her that God loves unconditionally, and the Brothers were the first to help her receive God's mercy.

She came to the charismatic Prayer group I led in the parish. She said she was drawn to me because of my faith. How humbling is that? For though both of us were far from being great examples of God's love, we saw His love in a real sense through the way we loved each other. If Paula was anything, it was "real". Nobody could get past her sense of BS. And she was quick to point it out, if she cared about you. I know, I tried.

Five

Overcoming past hurts

Forgetting the past

Paula also had to learn how to forgive. Her childhood was riddled with a lot of disappointments. One of the results of the life style she had lived, and the environment in which she lived in, was a need to eliminate bare bulbs. Growing up in the projects she had glass and rocks in the front yard, and a train switching yard in the back. The tracks were so close that she shook hands with the engineers. When I met Paula she was taking an interior decorating class to improve her life outlooks.

She seemed excited to be able to get so close to the trains, but I wonder what other thoughts were close to the heart and soul? I can only speculate that even if she never expressed it, perhaps she felt that she deserved better. The idea that we deserve better can poison our attitude for the rest of our lives. Her memories of the trains and the projects formed only one of many stories she told. But when she told them, they seemed to be wrapped in a coat of sweetness, revealing that even as a child, she was able to see the better side of adversities. If she was to share what she experienced during her hard times and her present home, she might say "don't worry. Be content and know that the God who created us loves us, he loves you right where you are and don't rush him. He will meet you where you are because he is already there.

Six

Transforming ideals into real life

Declarations and a rebirth through receiving God's love and forgiveness directly and profoundly impacts our daily lives. Paula lived out some of the ideas she had as well as the lessons she was learning. She strived to own them and live them out in practice. When we moved to California, we came to be with her daughter and son-in-law as they were having a baby. He was Paula's first grandchild.

When I met her and we were getting serious, she warned me that if any of her daughters were having a baby she would move, and leave me behind. She did not have to, for I too became papa to a wonderful boy, and Paula was NANA. She loved being Nana to all of her grandchildren. She was able to be around two of them here in California. I was blessed to be able to help her take care of them as her daughter and son-in-law worked. The following are some of the thoughts that she applied to in her role as full time caregiver and Nana.

Paula was concerned about her grandchildren's wellbeing, and she had the same frustrations that all people experience raising kids. She would struggle with wanting to be the disciplinarian and wanting to be a fun Nana also. She was both. She demonstrated how discipline could train our grandkids, and how rewarding it was to be able have fun with them. She really was a lot of fun. The challenges came when Paula and I would have difficult issues with each other to deal with. Then, the ideas she highlighted in the book that she gave me and these ideas gave her something to work for in those areas. She expressed how important it was to make sure the kids did not suffer because the adults were not behaving.

My own bad choices

It is with tremendous difficulty that I introduce the following subject: Our marriage was not always so good.

We made some bad choices, and eventually some of those choices led to our separation. In the end we were living in separate places. But I was with her as much as she allowed me to be me. One of my bad choices was to take on truck driving as a living. That choice was a result of a lot of other bad choices. But for the purpose of demonstrating Paula's tenacity in faith and love (and to encourage your own,) I will share highlighted passages that typify her effort during the hard times.

I can just hear her now, while I am in-time and she is not - "When negative things happen to us, no matter how much we yell and scream, murmur and complain, it's not going to make anything better." This truth was passed on from her lips to the any and all whiners, including myself.

Seven

The Victories

We had countless victories. That's normal, everyday life if you believe that God is in control, that He loves you, and you trust Him. I hope everybody finds this to become true in their lives, no matter where you are now in a relationship with Jesus. He brought many victories to Paula and myself.

I may add that we had our shared victories, and we had our own personal victories.

Some of my own were being able to meet Paula, get to know her, marry her and have nearly 10 years of marriage together. They were not easy, as I have revealed. What is a victory if there is no obstacle to overcome? I wonder if most of our obstacles are primarily of our own making, arising from our inner flaws. Paula, as perfect as she was, was still imperfect; and she knew it.

But as He so faithfully does, God used her most painful trials as a way of growing her faith and love. As the melanoma was eating away at her body, she became closer and closer to God. Because she recognized His hand upon her life, she was able to share with me some things that humbled her, yet could not shame her, a daughter of the King. She understood love better and better as she was getting closer and closer to PERFECT love. I have read about this happening in the hearts of other people who came close to passing out of this earthly life, some who we look up to as great role models. These people recognized their faults with profound humility. This can happen every day if we draw close to God. Our progress in love and holiness intensifies when a deadly disease is cutting an otherwise healthy person down. Natural bodies which house the sin nature but exposes our sin to the root of everything loving and lovely, our God and our savior exposing our true need for repentance.

16

Paula was fed by Joel Osteen and his family. This was evident in her devotional reading as well as in the story of Joel's mother. A survivor of cancer, she is still here by the faith and her releasing of the power of the Word. When she was able, Paula read the litany of affirming scriptures that was recommended by the Osteen's. She read them daily. When she was unable, I read them for her, many times in a day. I remember one time, as she laid in her bed, that she said she was going to live to be "an old lady". Knowing Paula, she meant an eccentric old lady. Curiously, God also used Paula's declining health to bring us closer to one another again. There was a true healing process working. We were able to see our own discrepancies and we were willing to chan8e for the better. We were willing to repent to each other as we both repented before God.

Eight

The "Big trip"

Preparations

This is a section of wonderful memories from our life together. I share them with you because, as with everyone, when we thought we were simply making our own choices, shaping our own days, and living our own lives, God was working out His plans for us, known from before He formed each of us in our mother's wombs. There is always so much more to life than meets the eye, and oftentimes we don't recognize this until our earthly journeys draw to a close.

Paula and I were well and happy in our married and shared life together in North Carolina. We both loved North Carolina, its culture of friendliness, the open spaces and the life in the country. We celebrated our life together, we struggled getting to know each other as we were living daily life as a couple. Her daughter from California was always in constant contact with her, and repeatedly asked when she was coming back to California. Paula loved North Carolina, but as stated earlier, she said from the very beginning of our relationship that if any of her daughters became pregnant she was going to them, (with or without me!).

One day we received an email from her daughter in California. In a word, she said she was pregnant. After receiving that information, we planned our departure from paradise. We both had to leave our jobs. We had one last get together of friends, said our good byes, and we were on the road.

The planning of that road trip, the circumstances of it, and the financial preparation for it were wonderfully smooth (for the most part). We had three vehicles between us.

She had her GMC Jimmy, I had a Plymouth breeze, and my favorite car of all time - a Mazda RX7. Paula drove her Jimmy to work, as we lived a long way from her job. I too had to drive a long way to work, but obviously only used one vehicle.

At work there was an international intern visiting us, and he was in need of a car to get around. I was able to loan my car to him at a better rate than the car rental companies. That was one resource of income. We also sold some of our stuff. The church we were attending helped us have a yard sale at the church, and afterwards we donated the rest of our stuff to the pastors. I was able to sell my beloved RX7 to a coworker. He was one of the few people who held up his end of the deals we made. We agreed upon a price and the conditions of the sale, and we both kept our word.

People did not always keep their word. We were preparing and making our arrangements. We needed money a moving truck, car hauler, a one-way plane ticket and expense money for an extended trip from North Carolina back to California. Paula was very organized, and she worked out a detailed budget of what was needed and when we needed to pay. Some of the folks we were dealing with on the other hand, were not so aware of our need to stick closely to that budget.

Our land lady had agreed to pay us back for an appliance that we bought for our trailer. The one she provided failed. In the end, she reneged on the deal, and in typical "Paula" style, we had a refrigerator, even if we dumped it on the side of the road on the way out. Not that Paula was mean or disrespectful. In fact, when we left the trailer it was in better condition than when we first arrived. That was Paula's way. She always said a deal is a deal.

The U-Haul and the plane

So after all the parties were finished, the travel arrangements were set, and everything was cleaned and packed, we started on a two legged trip from North Carolina to California. This is the plan we adopted. The first leg was a quick, nonstop trip straight to California in the moving truck and car carrier. We spent a few days visiting with her daughter, a lifelong friend, Connie, and unpacking. We left our car at Connie's home till we got back. We would then depart from Ontario, California airport to RDU airport. We would be picked up by a friend of ours, spend the night, and take off in Paula's Jimmy already loaded and prepared for a more extensive trip visiting family and friends. Indeed, the trip carrying most of our worldly possessions and our Plymouth Breeze went quickly.

We stayed in motels as we rushed across the country. We were always looking for deals along the way. Paula was so good about making sure things were right, and did not take it lightly when something was promised and not given. "A deal is a deal".

The way we would find our rooms was by looking at the discount books found at the rest areas. One of the main attractions for both of us was the ability to have a meal when we woke up, and not have to pay extra. "That was the deal!" Paula would say.

We were on a very tight budget and we needed all the cash we had to complete the trip. So one motel reneged on a proper breakfast, but you can be assured we did not go hungry, nor did we pay for the breakfast.

It was our custom to make sure we stopped at all the border rest stops. It was not only a way to truly rest, but also to get needed information to plan our trip, as we fine-tuned our plans along the way. You see, we didn't always take the freeway. Sometimes a two lane road was more appealing than the same old rush of trucks and straight pavement.

Most interesting were the history lessons and traditions of each state. Paula loved reading about the history of all the places we visited. I enjoyed the free coffee and the chance to sit and relax. Some of our gas stops were near tourist traps, and we also enjoyed getting a feel for the characteristics of the area by the stuff they offered. We always picked up spoons, for her collection.

The ribbon of light in the darkness and unknown destinies.

When we arrived in California it was dark. We stopped at the border road side rest as was our custom, but the usual welcome center was absent. In California you have to search for the welcome centers, and even if you find out what towns they are in, they are tucked away in places that camouflage their locations. It wasn't till nearly 10 years of living in California that I found one.

We stopped at the California rest area late after dark. While we were there, I discovered a trail that led out of the lights and into a dark place. I followed that trail and looked out to the road that was ahead of us. What a wonder! The land ahead was so covered in darkness. There wasn't a town, not even a porch light to be seen for, well it seemed forever. The only exception to that was the ribbon of white headlights and red taillights that cut a distinct line as far as the eye can seeThe stars were brilliantly bright in this vast desert sky and contrasted by a human marvel. In the deep darkness there was a trail of red and white lights cutting across the landscape. Everyone on that trail was going somewhere, who knows where? God knows. All this travel and going places under a vast darkness, but with a bright and shining jewel speckled sky, the very eye of God.

Only God knows what lies ahead of us in our darkness, in the comparatively small, yet long line of light we follow.

On this leg of our trip we visited her friend, (and maid of honor) in California. We didn't know that would be the last time they would see each other. Marcia Harcus was one of Paula's best friends since forever. She was the reason Paula came to North Carolina. Without their friendship Paula would never had the opportunity to be in paradise. Unfortunately Marcia's mother passed away, and she was with her brothers, after they buried her. It was unfortunate that Marcia lost her mom. But it brought another miracle of events for Paula.

We were able to visit with her and her brothers in Desert Hot Springs, California. This was the last time Paula saw her friend. We were going back to her home in North Carolina, but her boyfriend was the person we stayed with overnight. The highlight of this visit was when Paula woke me up before sunrise. I was so pleased that she did. She simply told me to follow her as we walked to the edge of the trailer court into the darkness (slowing turning to light). We saw beneath us the city lights, and as they were blinking off, the windmills became visible as the golden orb of the sun rose to meet us. We kissed, and she welcomed me to California.

Marcia was still in California on our turnaround leg. A few years after we were in our house, and Paula had beat the cancer the first time, she attempted to contact Marcia. She wasn't able to connect. She contacted Marcia's daughter and found out that Marcia had passed away from cancer. My poor Paula was devastated. Paula is so strong, but news like that hurt her deeply. Her strength and tenacity had two sides. She was a great joy to be around when she was happy, but the pain of life also reached as low as the victories reached high. Her strength and tenacity brought her to the land of doingthe-necessary, but there is the region of our hearts and mind that no one touches, the region in which we are transformed. Marcia touched that place. She loved Marcia.

Yet on this trip, what did we know about the last time, or even the new beginning? The image of the road in the dark keeps me grounded.

An extended trip with family and unanticipated goodbyes

We came to Riverside California the next day. Her daughter and son-in law were very busy people. They lived in a beautiful home with lots of bed rooms, a very large garage, and rooms that were larger than our entire trailer. After we unpacked the truck at the storage place, short visits and stored the car at Paula's friend Connie's home we were off to the airport.

Paula's Jimmy was packed and ready to go on a long trip, waiting for us in North Carolina. We were almost too late for a connection because our flight made us late. An entire plane load of folks were waiting for just Paula and myself. We arrived in North Carolina and Marcia's boyfriend met us at the airport. We stayed at their home overnight. They have two dogs - a large Doberman pincher and a small ankle biter. Paula loved animals especially dogs. She loved the contrast of the large dog and tiny dog. It was a picture her and myself.

We said good bye to our home, our country paradise, and she never went back.

The rest of the trip was a combination of various sleeping arrangements from the first night in the Jimmy, in a truck stop in Virginia. As we always did, we stopped at the rest stops, checked out the history, and moved on. We left in November 2003, and it was late November when we started the second leg. Driving through the mountains in West Virginia, we encountered snow, but only a light coating of the road. It wasn't until we arrived in Ohio that serious snow covered the roads.

The most remarkable memories of this time were mingled with parties in our honor, a theft of her purse, sleeping and bathing in so many different places and accommodations, and the sheer adventure. We spent Thanksgiving with my family (my dad's side) and I thought it was ironic that Paula had to sit with the "kids", myself being dad's kid. But Paula is 14 years older than me, and she was treated as a youngster. We had interesting times.

While we were at my mom's place there was a party in Paula's and my honor. A lot of folks came. Her purse was stolen while the party was underway. It was partly my fault. The weather was very cold. I thought I had locked the Jimmy, but it wasn't locked. Her purse and driver's license were gone. The outcome of that was that she did not want to take the chance of being pulled over without her driving license. So from that time on, I drove. It also held us back from our plans for half a day, as we had to report the stolen purse, and try to recover what she could. Ultimately it was all a waste of time. But Paula was very thorough about taking care of such details.

Every visit we had with each family member was distinct. We were blessed to have a warm welcome, and wonderful accommodations. They were simple many times, and the food they served was special, because we were with people who loved us, and even if the weather was cold the folks were warm. Paula was able to get to know my family for the first time and she appreciated more about "us".

It's notable that we went to see my mom's mom, my grandma in a nursing home. It wasn't an easy trip, as it took us longer to get to the destination we were trying to reach. We ended up getting to our destination very late, but it was worth it. My grandma had Alzheimer's disease. Paula and I were so blessed to find my grandma in a lucid state. She knew who I was, and she was able to meet Paula again. Little did we know, but we guessed that it was the last time to see her alive. I am so glad we made that last minute decision to see her, even if it was inconvenient.

Once we left Ohio we were on another stage of our adventure. We went to see friends of my own, and quickly they were friends of Paula. She was such fun woman, and everyone loved her. They liked her better than me, but it was my pleasure to introduce my own source of love and joy to the world.

On this trip we were able to spend some time with her daughter from St. Louis, Missouri. This leg of the trip was the most eagerly anticipated part of our "big trip". She missed being with her daughter so much. It was also the hardest aspect of this trip to leave her. The mother and daughter team had a wonderful time sharing the cooking, the sewing projects, the errands, and plain old ordinary life. We spent more time with her daughter than anybody else on this leg of the trip. We celebrated "Thanksmas". We missed Thanksgiving and we knew we would be in California on Christmas, so we had a holiday meal with a beautiful tree setting and tasty food, along with brand new sewing projects made by her daughter's hand to decorate the chairs. It was a hard day the day we had to leave. Paula loved her daughter very much and missed her when they were not together.

The open road and the beginning of the end of a trip.

As each new segment of the trip progressed, we realized that an end had been reached. We were no longer living as we were in North Carolina, and on this third portion both of our families and our friends were behind us. Now there was the new and unknown period ahead. As usual we took the side roads, and we travelled on historic route 66. To me there is something special about that period, and an adventure that is still being made. Paula too felt that sense of adventure. Whenever we could, she encouraged me to get off the freeway. She said she didn't want to be so close to the trucks.

But we weren't finished yet on this trip. After we left her daughter in Missouri, we had accomplished spending quality time with both of our families. Now we were genuinely "on the way" to our destination, to California.

We had adventures and we played the alphabet game a lot. The alphabet game was easy and it filled our time together. While you are traveling everybody involved looks around at signs, license plates, makes and models of cars, etcetera, looking for words or letters that start with "A". Then you progress till the winner is the first one to make it to "Z". It was a game that Paula taught me. She was very good at it. When we drove through areas that had little traffic, or no signs we used objects. A tree represented the letter "T".

On the way and on our last visit, we saw longtime friends of Paula's in Las Vegas. As time would tell, it too was a timely and wise stop. Joyce was only one of a few friends she truly loved. She worked with Joyce in the past in real estate. Paula was instrumental in getting Joyce and Gary together as a couple. There was a life change for Joyce and Gary. Eventually Gary lost Joyce to cancer, and Paula lost another friend due to cancer. We would talk about visiting them after we moved to California, but it never happened. It was the last time they were together. Gary was at Paula's memorial service as Paula and I went to Joyce's service.

After we left Vegas, of course, we took the side roads going through more desert and eventually landing in Riverside. California Our trip was over and a new life was starting.

We weren't in North Carolina anymore. But the memories and beautiful time we had was ultimately remembered toward the end of her life. We went on trips regularly after this. Sometimes our journeys were just up a hill, through a neighborhood that ended "somewhere", but who knows where? But we found our way. In the end she went on her own journey. With out me. The journey she started from her poverty, with all the ups and downs ended. Only those who know and trust Jesus will go on (or may even want to go on will go on) that journey.

Nine

Giving life and looking forward to the next

Giving platelets, giving life and Colby

Paula's tenacity was on display on a regular basis in many ways, one of them being her donation of platelets to the local blood bank. She was a donor before I met her, and she donated even with a busy schedule. Her jobs before she moved to North Carolina were as a paper lady, (early in the morning), caretaker, and a church secretary in the evening. She also sewed. But she always found time to donate platelets. She said that "they LOVED her platelets". And she loved to give, but it wasn't easy on her. She was 4 ft. 11 and a half. She was slim and trim. But donating made her weak from time to time. She would always get special attention because of complications, and when she donated I would pick her up from the center. She was wiped out after she donated, but as always she always sprung back up.

Later in life she was in dire need of a blood transfusion. The doctor we had at that time took better care of her than the other, and Paula was fading fast. She wasn't eating or drinking properly. It was common to go into the hospital emergency room to get hydrated. Yet the artificial hydration wasn't working sufficiently, and her blood was sluggish. After the visit we were encouraged to get a transfusion the next day, but unfortunately she was put off. We were put off another day and made an appointment for a Friday. We tried to get the preliminary work done the night before but she wasn't up to it. So that Friday morning, earlier than the appointed time I loaded her into the van. She was able to sit and be buckled in at that time. As we were driving to the hospital for this "emergency" procedure her phone rang, but we let it go to voice mail. She was unable to answer the phone. I was driving.

When we arrived and I loaded her into a wheel chair I pushed her into the waiting room. Please, let me explain that even when she was too weak to walk, her spirit was tenacious. She was on top of every situation. She had her barf tub, her drink, (that went mostly untouched), and her wits. Yet from my perspective it broke my heart to see a once active and strong woman suffering such severe weakness and fatigue.

When we were settled into the waiting room, she checked the voice mail. It was the very hospital we were sitting in. They called to postpone till Monday. Yep, put off again. But despite her weakness and fatigue she called the nurse back and she spoke to them. No, she would not let me take care of it. She called them and explained in no uncertain terms that she needed that transfusion. No it wasn't in a heavy handed, rude way that she handled the call. Once she would have done that, but this time, as she's crying tears too dry to come out, she told them that "I will not make it over the weekend. I'll be gone".

As I sit here writing this I have paused my typing. I don't know how to describe a moment like that. What can be said about a woman who is weak beyond compare, who is at the mercy of the health care system, and humbled to the point she has to beg for help? She was a woman that knew her situation and, by her own voice and actions, made the medical personnel give her the treatment she desperately needed. **She was tenacious**. She was bound to live and not die. She did not die that day, rather she was admitted and she received 2 units of blood, or platelets, or whatever she needed.

As you read this book I plead with you, as a blood donor myself, and a volunteer at the blood bank, to consider giving on a regular basis. It wasn't until I saw firsthand, - rather second hand - how much each donation means. I may add that we weren't the only people in this large room receiving donations. There are many who need just a little bit of what you have so much of. Paula gave to the point that it made her weak, but when she was weakened to the point of death she received life - life she gave to so many more.

She was scheduled to be put in a bed toward the rear of the ward. Perhaps they weren't convinced of her need over the phone. But when I wheeled her in she was placed in front of the nurses' station. The first bed. What happened after that in the ward was also life giving as the transfusion itself.

Prior to this episode our lives, I was introduced to a book called "Heaven is For Real". It was made into a movie later on. Anticipating this period of time in the ward,

I bought the book. As was the case usually in this stage of her life, I read to her. But let me make it clear, I only read what SHE wanted to hear, not just anything others thought she should hear. I read it out loud, obviously, but that being the case, it wasn't anticipated that I would be reading for everyone in earshot. The book spoke of a struggling family, a preacher that had a church, and a family. His son was misdiagnosed with deadly results. The child died, but came back to life and told some tremendous stories of his adventures.

For us, (Paula and myself) the story of Colby exposed us to what eventually was going to be Paula's experience, but not yet! But it did prepare both of us, each in distinct ways, for the possibility of what she was facing, and it was a joy! If she had any fear of dying before that reading, she did not have it then. For me it helped to let her go. One of the stories in the book involves a still born child. Paula had two. This topic is one of those that we keep close to our hearts, an event so profound we don't dare speak of it accept to report it, as a way to get to know a person, but unless you've been through it, there is no way another can know. Yet being her husband, I felt the pain and the joy of her experience, and of the loss, yet the joy that they were alive and waiting for their momma.

I was crying at these parts of the book. Yes, reading publicly and crying publicly, as she laid back quietly, soaking in the words of the book. She was receiving the gift of life (two units) and getting a new understanding of life (life after life.) She had me finish the book after we came home. She then wanted me to reread it another time shortly afterwards. She said once that she was getting ready to see her kids. The book is now a movie.

Giving blood and its products was essential to Paula in terms of getting the urgent treatment she needed, but that day both of us, and maybe others in the ward, came to see it from a different point of view as well. The secrets and human events we carry are important, but a spirit of tenacity and not giving up, here in-time as well as out-of-time, are connected. I see that better as I recollect the stories and adventures Paula and I have shared since Paula has been out- of- time. Let's see what we can be, as we too are tenacious, in our walks of life, and even if we are not doing it with the one we love, we can be assured that we can do it with the same Jesus that she was ready to see.

Ten

Another cancer

Carcinoid Syndrome

Carcinoid syndrome is a condition in which a carcinoid tumor secretes chemicals into your bloodstream. These tumors are rare and cancerous. They are usually located in your gastrointestinal tract or lungs. According to the National Library of Medicine, carcinoid syndrome only develops in one out of 10 cases of carcinoid tumors.

Yes another cancer was overlooked. We were concentrating so much on the melanoma that a second cancer developed in her intestines. The symptoms were what we expected from the melanoma, but they were very severe. If Paula was to eat even a very small portion of food or drink, she became very ill, and the pain would cause her not to eat even a small bite for days. The gas pains as she called them were so intense that she would merely lie there with a faraway look in her eyes. And you dare not touch her anyplace on her body. This too was a part of her tenacity. She did not give up despite the awful pain she was in and the severe weakness her body was suffering from lack of food and water. She was so determined that she was going to get help that she had me put her in the van and we were going to her doctor's office to get hydrated. No appointment, no chance of him turning her away once she arrived, right? Wrong, we did not have the chance to force the issue.

By the time she was able to get out of bed, (yes a major accomplishment) and to the medical center Paula was extremely worn out. I let the car at the curb, retrieved a wheel chair and put her in the chair. Usually Paula would wheel herself into the first waiting area, but she was still waiting for me by the curb when I parked the car. I wheeled her into the medical center, and into the elevator. When it started to go up, the elevator made a little more of a "jump" than usual, at least it felt like it as suddenly Paula's arms were flailed backwards and her head was as fallen back as it would go. Her eyes were wide open. It happened simultaneously as the elevator went up. She was staring into nothing.

I thought she was dead. I heard how people die with their eyes open and the way her body jerked I was in a panic. But I was able to operate the elevator and keep my attention on her, even if I was too busy keeping my eyes on her to even choose the floor level I needed. I was very much afraid.

As the door opened I wheeled her out, and called for help. I wheeled her right to the desk. I couldn't think of her doctor's name or any other thing accept to get help for her. They went right to work as soon as I wheeled her to the desk. By this time she knew her name, and where she was. I was so happy she was alive.

Thank God for Gloria.

There was another person who was with Paula as much and maybe more than myself. When I was at work her sister-in-law was a great source of help and she loved Paula very much. I made sure that she was involved most of the time. This was definitely one of those times. The medical staff was as good as they could ever be at that moment. She did not have to fight her doctor for care on that day. She was taken to the urgent care unit and taken a more direct way than we usually took. By this time she was surrounded by attentive nurses and doctors who took great care of her. She was hydrated after a long period of time, and she was her usual comical self again. Her doctor never did come by to see her. It was the last time we saw that doctor.

I wish so many times that I did not have to work during this period, but I did, so her sister-in-law accompanied her on another trip for hydration, but that time she went directly to urgent care, and it was the urgent care doctor that sent Paula to the emergency room. He saw what the problem was and that night she had emer8ency surgery. I have never seen a woman who is so full of spunk and energy look so weak. The staff must have not seen much like it before either as she was permitted to see the grandkids in her hospital room before she went into surgery.

All of her family that lived nearby and friends were in the waiting room. We truly had no idea if she was strong enough to survive a surgery. I was so focused on her that no one else mattered. I did try to make phone calls but I made a mistake by missing one call. I called her brother, thinking that he would be the same call as a call to her sister – in-law. Gloria. I was wrong about that.

I fell asleep in the waiting room and when I woke up, I was alone. Her friends went home, and her family was somewhere else, but I did not know where. I was only focused on one person. When I woke up I went to the desk, and they told me she was out, and in recovery. They let me go and see her. If I was thinking more clearly. I would have tried to find her daughter but I wasn't. I feel bad about that to this day. When I did see her she was awake enough to give a weak smile, and we held hands. I knew better than to talk.

She was alive!

Her family members did come and see her, and others came to her room later on. But I was so happy that she came around, and I called into work and took the next day off.

When she chased me away from the room, I slept in my car overnight so I would be able to see her as soon as I was able to. She survived the surgery and the cancer that tried to take her out early was dealt with. It wasn't long before she was on her feet again and eating and drinking well. She was gaining strength.

It was so good that she was still with us. For my part I left her alone with her family for a couple months. I was hoping she would call, but I figured she was happy to have her family from Missouri in California, and whenever she called me I would come to visit. I thought I was being sensitive by giving her space. We went on trips, and I took her to church, but there wasn't much else going on. I learned by accident that I was breaking her heart, (once again), by not pursuing her. It made for bad relationships with people that we knew and loved together, but there was also plenty of good times to remember.

Thunder, the grandkids and lost keys

There are plenty of positive stories that balance out the negative. After Paula was apparently well and on her way to recovery, we did see each other. One time was especially noteworthy, for it involved our dog Thunder, our grandkids and a funny twist that the kids and I will remember forever.

It was a nice autumn day and Paula and the grandkids wanted to see Thunder. Thunder is our golden Lab. The house I lived in was cat infested. Paula was allergic to cats. So in order to visit I took my usual walk to a prearranged destination. It is a dirt road in the middle of the city. We met and the kids and nana were excited to see

Thunder. Thunder was also excited to see the kids and nana. We had a great walk. At one point

Riley, my grandson and I separated from Nana and Reese. Riley and I wanted to climb a small but steep hill, but Reese and nana didn't. Riley, thunder, and myself had a good time climbing the rocks on the top and we went back down. When we got to the bottom Nana and Reese was gone.

After a few minutes we figured they changed their minds, and so we went back up again, to see if they were up on the top. Well, they did indeed change their minds and was at the top, but we was on the bottom of the hill while they were on the top. There are two ways up and down the hill. Of course we kept missing each other, but we finally did meet up, and we continued on the dirt road together.

When it was time to get back to the car, we decided to visit a friend and neighbor from our old house. What I discovered and what nana did not tell me was that she had accidentally fallen on her way up the hill. Naturally she picked up her cell phone, but forgot to pick up her keys. So we had a nice walk to see our friend, and he let us use a flash light and we walked some more to the hill. Our granddaughter, Reese was the first one to spot the keys. We had a good laugh, and a good time. Its times like this that I remember, even as I take thunder the same way, and I can see my wife and grandkids, even if only in my shared memory.

Eleven

Tenacious till the end

Stubborn

Paula had to take care of so much by herself for most of her life. It became a lifestyle. As mentioned, she sewed to overcome the lack of ability to buy clothes. She was very proud of one story involving a car repair. She fixed her transmission.

She asked a few people to help her, but they were not willing. She decided that she was going to fix the problem herself, despite any obstacle. She found out what the problem was, and took the bad part to the auto store. Naturally she had to walk and it was quite a distance. She walked the entire distance and walked back, got her hands dirty, and fixed the problem all by herself.

After she was divorced from her first husband she was single for 14 years. During those years she had to rely on her tenacious spirit, and when she did not know about something she wasn't shy about reading about it, learning, and then putting her new knowledge to work. All three aspects are important. How many times have I merely abandoned an idea because I was lazy? How many times have my opportunities been easy because they were already laid out and I did not have to work too hard? How many times did I not to try a little bit harder? I am still guilty, and I suppose Paula was too at times, but generally she did not give up. The result was that she knew a lot more about a lot of things, and I made the mistake of underestimating her.

Yet there were things that I was capable of, and I tried to help my wife out whenever I could. I would try from time to time to help her out on some projects, and problems she had. She was frustrated many times because of this or that, and she was a procrastinator in addition to the lack of time a day would offer. When she complained or mentioned an item of frustration out loud, naturally I wanted to come to her rescue!

I got into more trouble that way than any other. I would either not do it correctly (according to her way of doing it), or I was infringing on her space and project. It's true that I came from a background where in order to finish a project you could use a wrench as a hammer if a hammer wasn't available, and where I could recycle building materials rather than buy new and better material. But I finished the project, even if it was not professional. Paula was a professional about her work.

Sooner or later I learned to listen to her vent about her frustration, and merely listen. I would not try to suggest different ways, I would not volunteer to help. I did wait for the time she was ready for help, because at times she was ready for help, but I had to be patient.

The white picket fence.

One of her goals in life was to have a house with a white picket fence. We had lived in our house together a couple years and there was a flower bed next to the house and garage. Too many times it had become our grandson's personal construction site, or the dog's digging yard, so she decided to put a small picket fence around it, yes a white picket fence.

Her decision was made, so she waited, put it off, and finally got the materials. The material sat in the garage for a little while and she would piddle with it - take measurements, and look at the wood. We then bought more materials and she painted the individual pickets. She got busy on another project and when she came back, she measured the pickets for where she would drill holes. All the pickets had the same measurements. As time went on her daughter from Missouri was coming, and so she let me help her, if she was there to make sure I did it right. All I had to do was use a screw gun and screw the screws into the holes she made onto the cross wood, already measured out evenly spaced. After all the little fence spans were completed, I helped her measure the space we had to put it. She measured everything! And she completed that project, and it was level and straight. Years later the landlord still had that fence in the yard.

Hospice

Toward the end of her life she demonstrated that same kind of stubbornness, and demonstrated her inner strength, even when her body was weak. She was always using her senses as well as depending on herself as much as possible. This can be told in two different stories.

To many, hospice is the last part of life. Perhaps it is, but there have been cases where people have recovered enough to go home and live for many more years. But most of the time, it is the last stage, because at that point the options for treatment are not focused on healing the person. The goal of hospice is to make a person comfortable and wait for death. That can be helpful as families can attain closure, and love can be expressed as at no other time in life. But Paula wasn't closing anything. She knew that she was going to be healed. She knew that no matter how it looked, she was going to come out of her illness.

At the urging of friends and family she was asked to consider hospice. So she would let them come and see her. She knew that she needed help, but she also knew that hospice was considered the last resort. Hospice was not HER last resort. She knew she was going to beat the cancer with faith and God's power. The first time she flatly sent them away. Her physical existence was getting more painful and more difficult, so they came again, but she still did not take the care. On the third visit she did accept hospice. In my opinion she still knew she was going to get healed, but the medical community's rules gave her only one option - to get what she needed the most. She needed oxygen and a hospital bed. Period. The only way she was allowed to get oxygen was to take the entire package of hospice, which included a bed she needed and oxygen: but what she wanted to avoid was the high level of drugs that would incapacitate her ability to be on top of her body and her mind.

Fruit sickles

Paula was still convinced that she was going to live even after hospice. She demonstrated that by the way she nourished herself, and what she avoided. She avoided sugar at all cost. But she discovered a type of pop sickle that was nutritious, cold and hydrating. FRUIT sickles. It was sweet, comforted her, and hydrated her. As time went by she was getting weaker. One day she was given her fruit sickle and she was obviously struggling to pick it up and bring it to her mouth. As she was making a heart wrenching effort to feed herself one of her daughters attempted to help her. She merely reached over to steady her hand, but as soon as she did she was very quick with her free hand to slap the hand away. As we sat there and before anybody could say anything she spoke in the weakest voice I have head speak. She said "MYSELF". Everyone but myself had to leave the room. Her daughter who tried to help her commented on her stubbornness, and understandably, had to leave.

After everyone left I stayed. Just like the picket fence, just like so many projects, I supported her in her effort. I watched in wonder as she made the long trip to her mouth, well below the mouth, over the mouth, and eventually to the place where she consumed the rest of the fruit sickle. The next day she had another one, and she communicated that she wanted me to help. But that was the last fruit sickle she had. The drugs were affecting her body functions. She was becoming less able to manipulate. Eventually she was unable to talk. But she could still slap you away if she needed to. And her eyes were always alert. Her spirit never wavered

Twelve

The Even Bigger Trip

Life till Life

I recall being in her room, as I usually was when she visited with people. A friend who is a nurse had to break the bad news to Paula. There weren't going to be anymore treatment options coming from the medical community. Of course she still had hope that if she was able to continue with the hydration efforts, and blood transfusions, she would get better if only she could catch a breath of air, and therefore oxygen was what she wanted. But when her friend suggested there weren't going to be anymore treatments to fight the melanoma directly, she said that "I guess I am going to see Jesus". She was now ready to die, but to her it wasn't death; she was expecting to see a friend, a loving man who cared more than we can imagine.

Yet she wasn't entirely ready to give up. Her pain would cause her to drive everyone away. But she would call if she needed help. For my part I was with her whenever possible. I did have a job, but I would always be at her side, for as long as she would let me. We did not talk much. I sat with her and comforted her as she would allow me to. She loved to have her feet rubbed, and also wanted her legs and arms rubbed as well. I was an old pro at rubbing her feet. When she was healthy and we would be home at the end of the day, in front of the TV she would nudge her foot my way and my magic hands would work it over till she gave me her other foot. When she had enough of a massage she would let me know, and I would assume my seat and play Sudoku as she watched old reruns from the 70's and 80's on TV. If she needed anything I would fetch it for her. She enjoyed being read to. One of the books she enjoyed was *"Chicken Soup for Dogs"* If she needed her pillow adjusted I would help her.

One day I came to see her and she wasn't in the bed. I looked in the bathroom, but she wasn't there, and the kitchen but she wasn't there. So I went back to her room and she had fallen off the bed but was on the far side of the bed. She greeted me with a smile and proceeded to explain how she came to be on the floor. She told me that she was relaxing, trying to adjust a bit and "swoooop" she was on the floor as she was laughing about the entire episode. She was unable to get up on her own, but she was unhurt, and patiently waiting to be discovered. I picked up this woman I loved, and put her back into place.

The profundity of our intimacy and love grew in ways that I cannot describe. I can't because they were too personal and also because you have to be in a position of desperate events to test your love. If you haven't been there, you won't understand. In some ways I hope you never do. But if you are ever in that situation, I hope you are strong enough to do what you need to do. The reward of merely being with the one you love, and assisting them is overpowering.

"Who is she waiting to see?" (Hospice nurse)

As time went by, she got weaker and weaker. There were times that I was sure she was "going to-see Jesus." She had a certain stare into nowhere, and at the same time, someplace that I could not see. I figured she was on a trip that I could not go with her.

But even when she was in that condition she was able to let me know if I was welcome, or if she needed to be alone. She wanted to be alone more often than she wanted company. One day I left her side to come to where I lived for a short break. It only took a few minutes before I got a call from her. She wanted my company. It was the last call I received from her. But generally it was her direct family, a few personal friends and myself that she wanted to be around. Ironically she was surrounded by a lot of caring and beautiful people on her last day, but by this time she wasn't able to protest.

The hospice nurses were coming to see her for the first time. They visited with her and were going to plan a strategy of care. One look from the nurse prompted her to ask a profound question. What is she waiting for? Who does she want to see? This properly alarmed her daughters and phone calls were made and the entire house was crowded with people who wanted to say good bye, or to console her Family. The Hospice Chaplain came and a service was provided. The service was very emotional as we came to the realization that she was ready to see Jesus. By this time she was unable to talk, so she wasn't able to tell us if she wanted to be alone or not. For my part I checked in on her but did not stay in her room, as there was a constant flow of well-wishers and love that needed to be expressed in private. But I knew she wanted to be left alone. That's what she said when she was able to talk. Some folks were talking to me as well, but mostly I took care of her physical comfort, keeping her comfortable, and planning her rose garden event.

By this time her final arrangements were made, and they were what she wanted. She made sure she conducted her business, but it was her eldest daughter who did the leg work, and it was difficult for her daughter and family. She was living with them in her own room and took care of the grandkids as much as she could. The grandkids helped her more toward the end as they would spend time with their nana watching TV and checking in on her during the day. It was told to me that they would go see her before they left the house and she blessed them by saying "God go with you".

Her final arrangements were as giving as she was always in her life. She donated her body to science. Even as I write this, she is helping a future doctor in an anatomy lab. We will receive her ashes on the second anniversary of her homecoming. Those were her wishes. The second set of wishes that she told me about concerned her service - a rose garden event.

When she was filling out the paperwork for her service arrangements she merely said that her friend and pastor would know what to do. But she also arranged with another friend for a ceremony he does for the living. Paula had a written list of names of people she was influenced by and loved. After she went to life –eternal she wanted them to know how much and why they were special to her. That pastor came to see her and he was able to get an idea of why these people were selected to receive a ribbon and a single rose. Thus the Rose Garden ceremony.

The day people came to say good bye was her last, and in the early hours of the next day she said her good bye to the three of us standing by her bed side. For my part, she showed me that she loved me in a tangible manner. I saw her move her eyes toward both her daughters. It looked as if she was trying to communicate with them. The presence of another person was strong, and even if I could not feel that person I knew Paula saw Him. After she was looking at her daughters she gazed directly at me, and with as much strength as she had when she was strong she grasped my hand and squeezed it tightly, and she was gone. In my hope that I was wrong I wet her lips, as she seemed to breathe so shallowly for so long, but she was gone. I miss her very much.

Thirteen

Out-of-time

Paula was a great assistance to me after she "went to see Jesus" in dream. I will use a story that combines her spirit, and our love of dancing. For it was our love of dancing that brought us together after we were separated by eternity, temporarily.

Contra dancing

Years before I met Paula I was very active in a contra dance community. One of the ground rules of the dances is that you change partners as much as possible. It was safe way to take a woman out and I would not have to call it a date. Routinely if I asked a lady to a dance I qualified it as "not a date". So soon after I met Paula I asked her to go dancing with me, and of course stated that it was not a date. She came with me and she came many times more, but the more time we spent together, the more I broke the rule of not dancing too much with Paula. I qualify that by saying I did not want her to be standing alone, but if she had another partner for any sequence, I let her go.

The dance is a lot of fun, filled with a room full of endorphin high dancers. It is country, yet sophisticated and the musical bands were always tremendous. The callers were patient and helpful. The community, as we called ourselves, was friendly. We met every week, sometimes 2-3 times a week. It was very friendly, so naturally Paula fit right in. We loved to dance together.

The dance moves are similar to square dance moves, but contra has a few of its own. I remember my sweet wife taking a form and just making it wonderful. That was the move called a gypsy. It was dancing with a person, as if you were swinging them, but you did not touch them. You simply go around in circles "gazing" into the other person's eyes. Intense right? It's as if to say, you can look, but you can't touch. My Paula had her own twist on that. As she was circling she would "wiggle". Adding a sense of humor and an accent that says, not only can't touch me, but here, "la-la-la".

Dancing was a natural connection for us. She was a natural, and we were both free spirited. We were always the first to the dance floor. But we didn't need a band or a "dance floor". You might catch us dancing in the aisles of the grocery store, the hardware store, or anyplace that music was played. We even had a few dances in the privacy of our home.

The dream

Remembering these dances helped me to remember a dream I had of her after she went to see Jesus. I dreamt that I was at the bottom end of a long and great theater. The seats were packed, and a show was on. Everyone was watching. At that moment I "sensed" her presence and knew where she was. But she was there and I was here, so I felt self-conscious about interrupting her in heaven but then some music played. Yes music. And so I left the front of the auditorium/theater and ran up the aisles, but she was way in the back, but not in the back row. I "felt" I made contact with her, as her.

"She" (whatever form she was in,) was pushing past the people to get out of her seat.

She met me in the aisle and we went running to the dance floor. But the music ended. We were at the stage/dance floor, in plain sight of the entire crowd, but I did not notice them anymore. All I saw was Paula. We watched a side show of a corn farmer whose corn was all bad. It was cancerous. The farmer was broken up with grief. It was all he had. And he had another crop that was liquid, and it too was sour. We both looked at each other and decided that this was too depressing, so I chased her up the aisle, yes folks were watching us, and out the door in the back. We crossed over a lawn and I chased her to a swimming pool. As I got into the entrance I saw there was a clear glass partition between us. I couldn't reach her, she was so close yet so far. I spoke and said I was going to swim around to her. I was determined to get to her.

Give me a moment...

She spoke to me. I heard her voice for the first time in months. What she said was typical Paula fashion. She asked me if I should, ("maybe someone is using it"), but the voice was not the same tone as she might use in time. This is what I am trying to convey through this story. Her voice was melodic, entirely absent of stress, of worry, and pain.

I would say happy, or peaceful, but those terms don't touch the meaning of what I am trying to say.

The dream ended. But the reassurance of her state in heaven, in the presence of her true love, Our God, our Savior, and our true Daddy will always make even my hard days tolerable.

Fourteen

Faithful friend and pastor.

Paula could literally count the people she considered real friends on one hand. She lost a couple while in California, and so the few she has she treasured. Connie was one and was faithful to Paula. Kathleen was another friend and I found out after Paula past how much she was a friend to myself.

Kathleen was a friend we discovered "by accident". Many years before I met Paula she was married and raising a family in California. Her husband at the time was in a band. Kathleen was also married and raising children, and she was a part of Paula's husband's band. There came a time when Paula was extending her hospitality and help to Kathleen. They grew to be great friends, confidants, and sisters. That was nearly 25 years before I met Paula. As many know such friendships don't change, but time changes us.

After Paula and I moved to California, and while we were living in with her brother, we started to attend a neighborhood church. We went for a couple times and eventually invited Kathleen and her family out to eat. We had a terrific time, so we did it again the following week. We were introducing ourselves slowly and talking around the table when a light bulb went off in both Kathleen and Paula. THEY KNEW EACH OTHER.

From that time on Paula and Kathleen never separated. Kathleen remarried and we were at the wedding, and after they started a new church, Paula and I were one of the first members. We did a lot of work to help the new pastors. Paula and myself help set up for special events, parties, and the food pantry. Eventually we were ordained as ministers.

Paula and Kathleen grew very close. When Paula had no one else she could share her frustrations, her hurt, and what life threw at her she always had Kathleen. Sometimes Paula was supported in her struggles, but sometimes Kathleen would gently correct her. I found this out after Paula went to see Jesus, but I also figured it out before. When we went to church in the morning Paula would sometimes be distant. She was experiencing those thought- too- close to her heart to share. But after the service and a long time after the service Paula would be talking to her pastor, and magically Paula was friendly again, even if it was a restrained warmth.

After Paula was ready to see-Jesus she told me she had talked to her friend and pastor about her final arrangements. She in fact tried to, but Paula's friend was not giving up.

She was suggesting this and that treatment, and we went along. There was also a time that the pastor's presence in life is the only one that was needed. Pastor Kathleen was not able to come, so her husband pastor Richard came. That same night Pastor Benjamin also came. He was the friend who had the Rose Garden ceremony.

Pastor Kathleen was unable to see her friend while she was sick. Paula totally understood. They had an understanding. Yet what pastor Kathleen and Richard did for her, for her family, and for me was an act of love. They had Paula's memorial service. The service details were mixed with the visiting pastor Benjamin's rose ceremony, and of course the arrangements made by Kathleen and myself. Special shirts imagined and created by her daughter in St. Louis was printed by members of Kathleen's family. They stated "I wear Black for Paula" with a melanoma ribbon. The back had a small black ribbon on the spot that it all started.

For my part I am not only I indebted to Kathleen and Richard financially, but also as a friend. They currently have a special place in their church with a picture that Paula and I shared in life. The picture has tall majestic mountains in the background, a lake in the foreground, and deer panting from the water. It was one of the few items that survived from bachelor years. The picture and a small table with pictures of Paula, her church recognitions, and flowers are always present. It's one of the few places that has a small shrine for a beautiful friend, Kathleen's friend and my wife, Paula Forbush.

A testament to Paula's friendship was how I would continue to attend the church again, but not always on a regular basis. My attendance for a year after the memorial service was remarkably coincidental. I always took flowers when I went, and sometimes Paula would send me to church with flowers for other occasions. That first year I went on both birthdays of the pastors, their wedding anniversary, the churches anniversary and time when members of the church had sad or happy life events. I personally did not, nor do I know presently, the pastors birthdays and anniversary. When I felt an inclining to go I knew it was for a purpose.

Hurry honey, hurry

Paula and I communicated a lot the first year after she went to see Jesus. One such story is a tremendous example of how she was still connected to her church. The story also involves a sad story of my separation from Paula's loved ones. But in the end everything works out, and it's that hope and tenacious faith that she had, that I share.

Her brother was in the hospital and from what I heard he was dying. He was dying of the same cancer of the intestines that Paula had. Unfortunately I was a part of that. But Paula used her tenacity and my connection to her to help out a church member. I did not have a car, but I had a bike and so after work one day while her brother was deathly ill, I heard her tell me that I needed to go to the hospital very quickly. so I rode and on the way I heard her say, emphatically, Hurry honey, hurry!. I was certain her brother was a goner.

When I arrived at the hospital I found out that I was not permitted to see my brother-inlaw. No one of her family wanted to see me. I was hurt because Gloria was such a great help, I wanted to help her. So I went to the chapel and I prayed for Richard, and for the family. I found out later that my brother-in-law recuperated enough o go back to teaching. Praise the Lord.

What happened next is a miracle. As I was leaving I saw a young girl from our church. She was sitting alone and crying. naturally I went up to her and she explained that she was waiting for her ride, but that she had just, moments ago, lost her boyfriend. The timing of my ride, of the prayer in the chapel, and her coming outside was God's timing. It was also a testament that Paula was and is a part of her church and even if she could not be there, she used me to convey her love.

Fifteen

The conclusion

Life in God is even fuller of history and mystery - history that begins with Him and never ends, and the mystery of how He dwells within us. The greatest mystery is and how the same God who gives use mortal flesh and knows the number of days in our earthly lives, also prepares a place for us to live for all eternity (no rest areas needed), and bodies that do not die.

In the beginning, we are born into life on earth. At the end, we are born into life in heaven. Though not very much was the same for Paula and me at the end, as compared to the beginning - one thing was - We were together, we loved one another, and we knew that love was stronger than death.

As I look back over our years together, I can begin to see some of God's larger tapestry -

We were together to be Ken and Paula for 12 years, but we were also together to walk toward eternity and look beyond even all the fullness this life can bring, to the One that is so much fuller. We were together to learn that pain and suffering are stepping stones to compassion, wisdom, and grace. And we were together so that I could share our lives with you, so that perhaps you will be moved to look beyond the particular experiences of each day, or the particular hand you may feel life has dealt to you, to the vastness and fullness of blessing that God has for you - plans to give you a future and a hope.

May He bless you now and always.

Printed in the United States
by Baker & Taylor Publisher Services